SPICE GIRLS SPICEWORLD

GW00566940

Wise Publications
London / New York / Sydney / Paris / Copenhagen / Madrid

Exclusive Distributors:
Music Sales Limited
8/9 Frith Street, London W1V 5TZ, England.
Music Sales Pty Limited
120 Rothschild Avenue, Rosebery, NSW 2018, Australia.

Order No. AM953095
ISBN 0-7119-7078-5

Visit the Internet Music Shop at
http://www.musicsales.co.uk

'Spice Up Your Life' arranged by Roger Day.
All other music arranged by Derek Jones.
Music processed by Paul Ewers Music Design.
Poster photograph courtesy of Adrian Green.

Printed in the United Kingdom by
Printwise (Haverhill) Limited, Haverhill, Suffolk.

Your Guarantee of Quality:
As publishers, we strive to produce every book to
the highest commercial standards.
The music has been freshly engraved and, whilst endeavouring
to retain the original running order of
the recorded album, the book has been carefully
designed to minimise awkward page turns and to make
playing from it a real pleasure.
Particular care has been given to specifying
acid-free, neutral-sized paper made from pulps which
have not been elemental chlorine bleached.
This pulp is from farmed sustainable forests and
was produced with special regard for the environment.
Throughout, the printing and binding have been
planned to ensure a sturdy, attractive publication
which should give years of enjoyment.
If your copy fails to meet our high standards,
please inform us and we will gladly replace it.

Music Sales' complete catalogue describes
thousands of titles and is available in full colour
sections by subject, direct from Music Sales Limited.
Please state your areas of interest and send a
cheque/postal order for £1.50 for postage to:
Music Sales Limited, Newmarket Road, Bury St. Edmunds,
Suffolk IP33 3YB.

SPICE UP YOUR LIFE

Words & Music by Victoria Aadams, Emma Bunton,
Melanie Brown, Melanie Chisholm, Geri Halliwell, Richard Stannard & Matt Rowe

When you're feel - ing sad and low, we will take you
Yel - low men in Tim - buk - tu, col - our for both

where you got - ta go. Smil - ing, danc - ing, ev - 'ry - thing is free,
me and you. Kung - fu fight - ing, danc - ing queen,

all you need is po - si - ti - vi - ty. Col - ours of the world, ev - 'ry
tri - bal space - man and all that's in - be - tween. (Spice up your life.)

boy and ev - 'ry girl. Peo - ple of the world,
(Spice up your life.) (Spice up your life, ah!)

4

STOP

Words & Music by Victoria Aadams, Emma Bunton,
Melanie Brown, Melanie Chisholm, Geri Halliwell, Paul Wilson & Andy Watkins

1. You just walk in, I make you smile. It's cool but you___
(Verse 2 see block lyric)

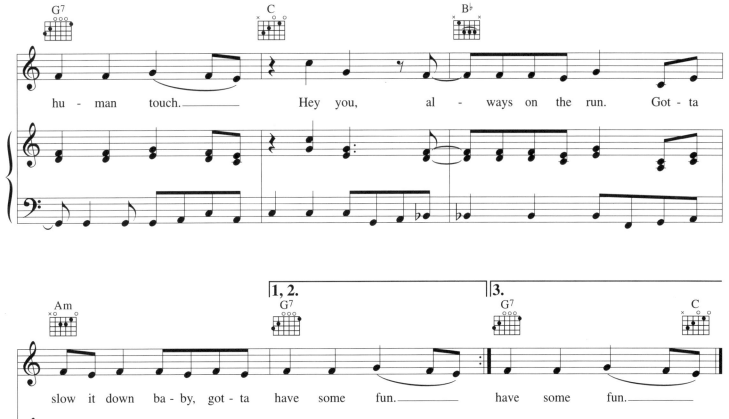

Verse 2:
Do do do do
Do do do do
Do do do do, always be together.
Ba da ba ba
Ba da ba ba
Ba da ba, stay that way forever.

And we know that you could go and find some other
Take or leave it 'cos we've always got each other
You know who you are and yes you're gonna break down
You've crossed the line so you're gonna have to turn around.

Don't you know *etc.*

TOO MUCH

Words & Music by Victoria Aadams, Emma Bunton,
Melanie Brown, Melanie Chisholm, Geri Halliwell, Paul Wilson & Andy Watkins

1. Love is blind— as far as the eye can see,— deep and mean-ing-less
(Verse 2 see block lyric)

Verse 2:
Unwrap yourself from around my finger
Hold me too tight or left to linger
Something fine, built to last
Slipped up there, I guess we're running out of time too fast.

Yes, my dear you'll know he soothes me (moves me)
There's no complication, there's no explaination
It's just a groove in me.

Too much of something *etc.*

SATURDAY NIGHT DIVAS

Words & Music by Victoria Aadams, Emma Bunton,
Melanie Brown, Melanie Chisholm, Geri Halliwell, Richard Stannard & Matt Rowe

Get down, deep-er and down,— get down, get deep-er and down.— 1. I'm not a-lone,

now you're not in my mind,—   you were the vic-

(Verse 2 see block lyric)

-tim of— your crime,— I left you be-hind.—   Boy,— you were a fool

to treat me that   way,—   I'm not gon-na let—

19

Em7   Am7

_____ you, I'm gon - na for - get____ you, there's no-thing to say.____

Cmaj7   B7

You're a twist - ed lov - er,_____ kiss and tell - in' on___ a su-

Em7   G/D   A7

- per - star,____ that's what you are._____ Well it was

Cmaj7   G   B7

Sa - tur-day night, I know the feel-in' was right, I did-n't know we'd get___ so far.____

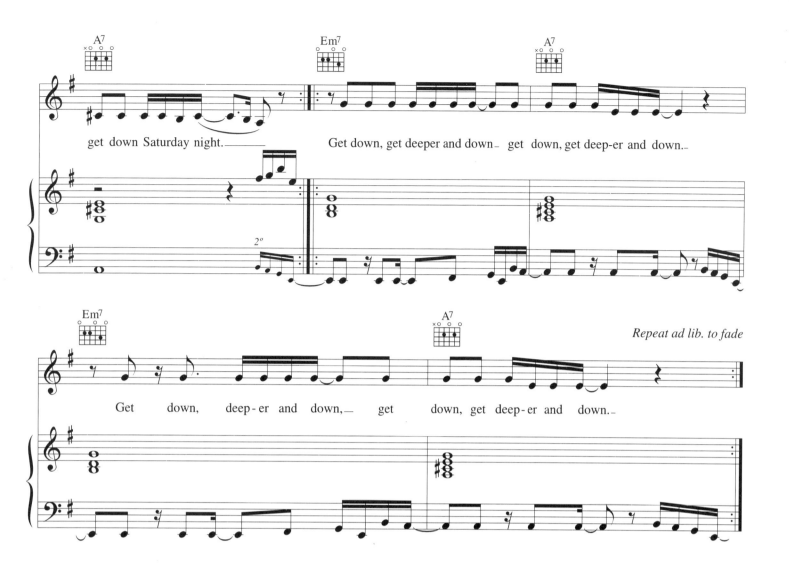

Repeat ad lib. to fade

get down Saturday night._____ Get down, get deeper and down_ get down, get deep-er and down._

Get down, deep-er and down,_ get down, get deep-er and down._

Verse 2:
Take it from me
You know I mean what I'm saying
You'd better watch out
You'd better wise up to mind games he's playing.
He may have the looks
He may have the charms
But where does he go
What does he do when he's not in your arms?

Keep your head up high
Don't you know you are the superfly
And that ain't no lie
But it's a Saturday night
We got a feelin' that's right
Don't you know we'll get so high.

Get down, get deeper and down *etc.*

NEVER GIVE UP ON THE GOOD TIMES

Words & Music by Victoria Aadamo, Emma Bunton,
Melanie Brown, Melanie Chisholm, Geri Halliwell, Richard Stannard & Matt Rowe

1. She

used to be — a chan-cer, spark - le in the rain, — told me she need - ed a friend.

(Verse 2 see block lyric)

If she's go-ing cra - zy, ba-by's on the way, —

seems like the day — nev - er ends. — Ev-'ry-bo-dy needs some af - fec -

- tion, — nev - er shines, got-ta try, wher - ev - er you're go - ing.

3. Down and dir-ty ci - ty feel - in' out of place,

may- be you've ran ___ out - ta time. ___ He treats her like a la - dy, a

smile up-on her face.— Make up the last_____ of the lines.—

Ev - 'ry - bo - dy needs some af - fec -

- tion,_____ nev-er shines, got-ta try, where - ev-er you're go - ing.

Nev - er give up on the good times, got - ta be - lieve in the love you

Nev - er give it up, no. Nev - er give up on the good times,

find.— Nev - er give it up, no.

liv-in' it up is a state of mind.—

Nev - er give it up, no. Nev - er give it up, no.

Repeat ad lib. six times

N.C.

Hey now, look a - round,— pick your - self up off the ground.— I said

Nev - er give up on the good times, got - ta be - lieve in the love you

29

Verse 2:
Bossanova baby, heart is never soul
Shouting but he's never heard
Eyes all wide and open, the streets are paved with gold
Someone come back on their word.

Everybody needs *etc.*

DENYING

**Words & Music by Victoria Aadams, Emma Bunton,
Melanie Brown, Melanie Chisholm, Geri Halliwell, Paul Wilson & Andy Watkins**

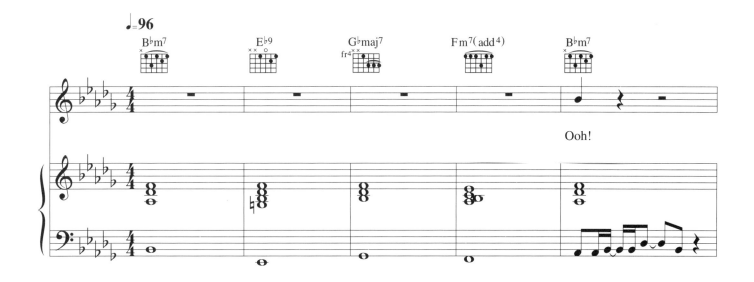

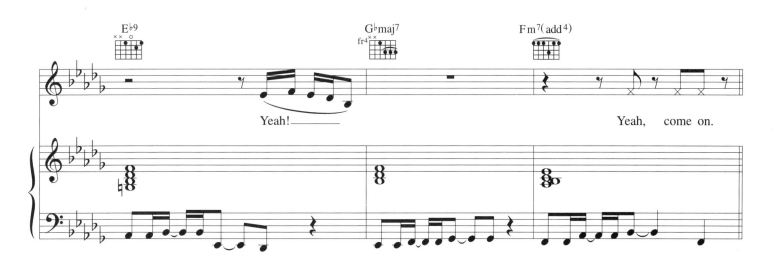

MOVE OVER

Words & Music by Victoria Aadams, Emma Bunton,
Melanie Brown, Melanie Chisholm, Geri Halliwell, Mary Wood & Clifford Lane

Next phase, next stage, next grade, next wave.

Let me tell you 'bout a thing got-ta put it to the test, it's a ce-le-bra-tion, mo-ti-va-tion, ge-ne-ra-tion
Well

next.
sow me the seed,— ev-'ry col-our ev-'ry creed. Teach, nev-er preach, lis-ten up and take heed.

Take the heat,— feel the flow, cos you're rea-dy to burn— and we're rea-dy to go.—

got-ta know the rules if you wan-na play the game. Re-spect and de-di-ca-tion nev-er rhyme on the phone.

Dedication!   Good vibration!   Baby nation!
Celebration!   Motivation!   Recreation!   Crazy nation!   Move
Anonimation!   Domination!   Imagination!

ov-er,   yeah,— don't do it ov-er.   Cos it's ov-er yeah,— yeah, yeah..

—— Move ov-er, yeah,— don't do it ov-er.   Cos it's

DO IT

Words & Music by Victoria Aadams, Emma Bunton,
Melanie Brown, Melanie Chisholm, Geri Halliwell, Paul Wilson & Andy Watkins

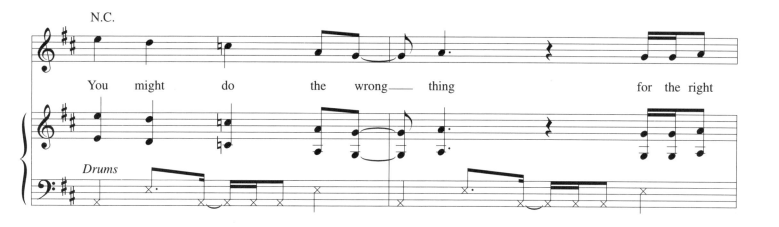

You might do the wrong——— thing for the right

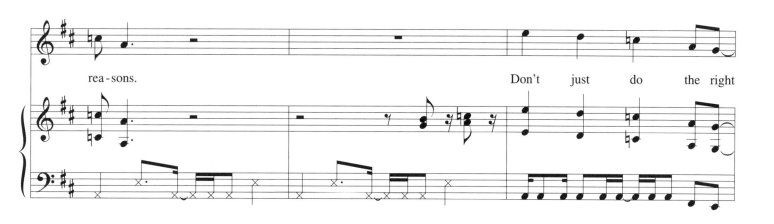

rea-sons. Don't just do the right

D.%. *Repeat Chorus to fade*

——— thing to be pleas-in'.

Drums

Verse 2:
Remember things like you should be seen and never heard
Give a little respect to me and it will be returned
Keep your head down, keep your nose clean, go back against the wall
Girl there's no way out for you, you are sure to fall.

Who cares what they do because it's yours for the taking
So, it's not for you anyway, make your own rules to live by.

Come on and do it. *etc.*

VIVA FOREVER

Words & Music by Victoria Aadams, Emma Bunton,
Melanie Brown, Melanie Chisholm, Geri Halliwell, Richard Stannard & Matt Rowe

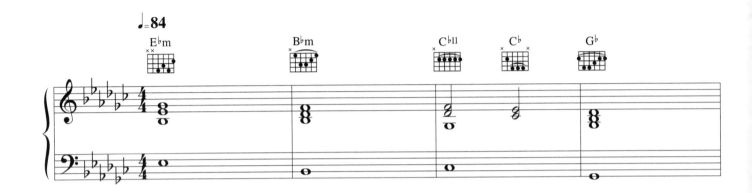

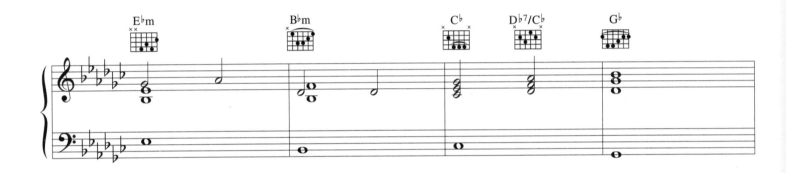

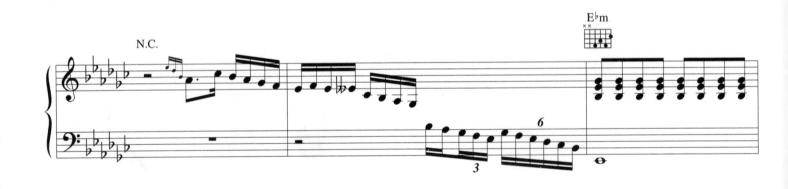

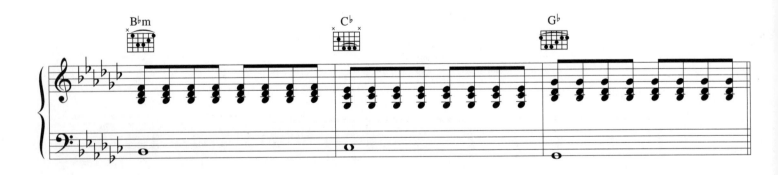

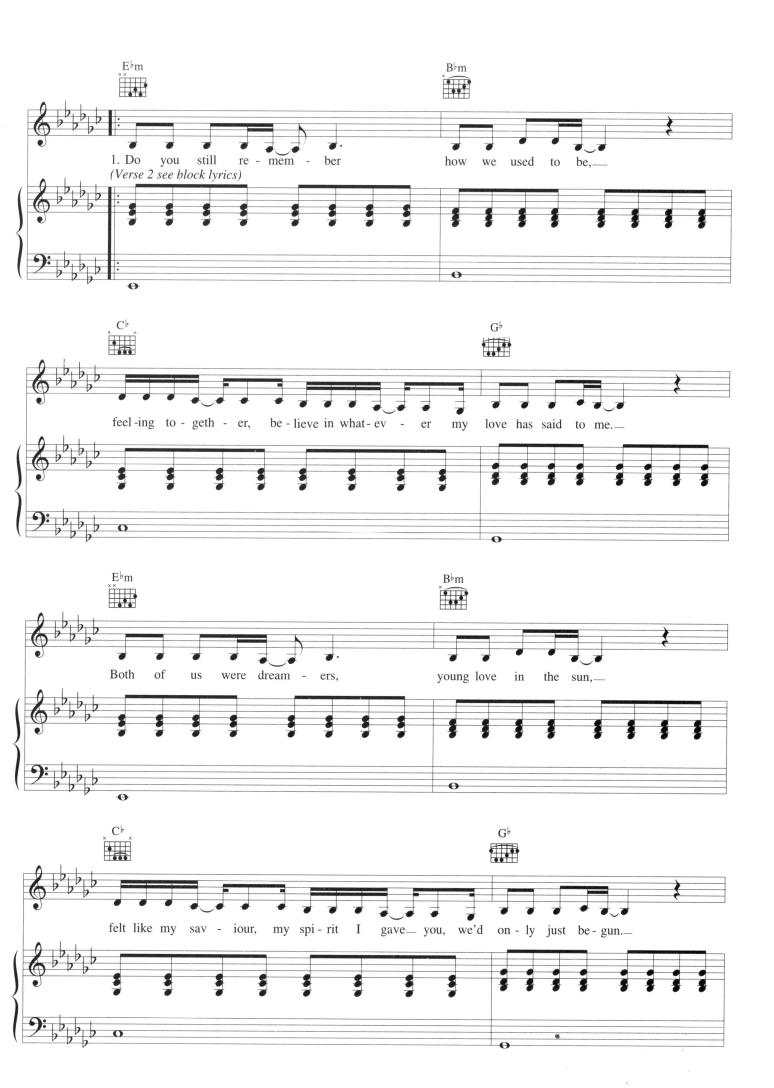

Back where I be-long— now, was it just a dream,-

feel-ings un-fold, they will nev-er be sold and the sec-ret's safe with me.—

Has - ta— man-an-a,— al - ways — be mine.

Vi - va for-ev - er,— I'll be wait - ing,— ev-er-last-

Verse 2:
Yes, I still remember, every whispered word
The touch of your skin, giving life from within like a love-song that I'd heard
Slipping through my fingers like the sands of time
Promises made, every memory saved, has reflections in my mind.

Hasta manana *etc.*

THE LADY IS A VAMP

Words & Music by Victoria Aadams, Emma Bunton,
Melanie Brown, Melanie Chisholm, Geri Halliwell, Paul Wilson & Andy Watkins